my lungs
are a
dive bar

(some)other books by EMP

my lungs
are a
dive bar

for bill hicks & townes van zandt
in honor of *paris, texas*

walter moore

Toledo, OH
http://www.empbooks.com

First Edition

ISBN: 978-0-9997138-4-6
LOC: 2019934895
10 19 33 34 6 11 1973

Design, Layout, and Edits: Ezhno Martín

Cover Art/Photo/Pool Of Folly: Grant Whipple

"the man who publishes a book without an index ought to be damned ten miles beyond hell, where the devil could not get for stinging nettles"

— **john baynes (1758-1787)**
(we're fucked)

"if jesus don't like jimmy carter . . . he needs to read that book"

— **patterson hood**
(side comment, solo show)

*in case it wasn't obvious, there is no
table of contents
fortune favors the bold
turn the page*

billy collins

went to a poetry reading in
indiana given by billy collins

he is a funny bald man
and
i enjoyed what he had to say

he worked the room

after the reading all us kids
met up with collins
at a dive of a bar called
the duck

billy really put the drinks back
and
i think he was hitting on
my girlfriend

i had a nice conversation
with him about writing
and baseball

later on in the night billy found
himself at my friend slabaugh's house

we call slabaugh *balls*

there were a handful of us
there

balls has a large brown dog
and
billy was wrestling with it

at one point in the night billy was
on all fours barking like a dog
himself

i'd always wanted to meet a poet laureate

i count my blessings before i sleep

thanks for the rose made of
bamboo
you bought me in vietnam
for driving my car into
the woods and totaling it in
tulsa

thanks for breaking my hand
in houston
thanks for pressuring me
to pick you up
from prom
even though i was on
house arrest

for nearly drowning me in
indonesia
for cheating on me with moby

thanks for going into the
mental hospital without telling me thanks
for moving away

for dying
then coming back to life

for ripping me off
every holiday

progressive

my tattoo
artist is my guru
i go to him for
wisdom advice
even when i
don't need a tattoo

for example i
have a stupid
rose tattoo
because i couldn't
come up with a
better idea
but i wanted to hear
a parable
from him

one anecdote
involves damon
(his name is damon)
monkey mouthing a
neo nazi

damon has founded an organization
in north central indiana that
tortures neo nazis

                they recently preyed
            on a neo nazi rally
                    left a few
            nearly dead
    he says the police didn't care
            kind of encouraged it

                    "i monkey
            mouthed that
                    motherfucker
            hit my gun
                    into his mouth
            so hard fucking
                    fascist cried
            like he was sucking
                    on his mom's
            rib cushions"

                    what wonders
            my rose
                    looks sublime
            a symbol for
                    monkey mouthing
            for getting it all right on skin
                    for believing in
            something
    better than you think
            somewhere between
                    the street and
            god
                    damon and his
            justice acts
    i keep learning

neighborhood

smoking cigarette front porch before noon monday. i see hear young couple cross way front of small apartment complex. she: "i'm tired of you talking to me like that. tired of this shit." he: "you ain't should be talking to me like that" she: "you fucking yelling at me for smoking cigarettes. you smoked all the damn cigarettes. that cigarette is the first one i got." he: "bitch, shut the fuck up." he throws something small in the direction of her back. they both walk inside the apartment, shut their door, i yell: "i have cigarettes! you can have some of my cigarettes!" they don't hear me because they are inside and i am outside. maybe i should go knock on their door, offer my cigarettes. i imagine the possible responses: (1) "thank you, that was nice of you to come over here and offer your cigarettes." or (2) "bitch! we don't want your cigarettes. put a shirt on motherfucker!" as a neighborhood compromise, i throw a cigarette into the middle of the street, roughly equidistant from my front door and their front door. i wonder which one of us will smoke that cigarette later? maybe the 15-year-old lawn boy who injects heroin before he mows my lawn will pick it up, smoke it before starting the mower but after he has injected heroin. my community is very important to me.

jo h: part 2

my 15-year-old lawn boy johnathan or jo h nathan as
i call him consumes heroin. no joke. a person might
write "my 15-year-old lawn boy injects heroin" when
they really mean "my 15-year-old lawn boy (here in
the suburbs, for example) *is complicated.*" my lawn
boy jo h does heroin. on a regular basis. we have fun
conversations about it. i give him the warnings you
would expect though: i warn him it is not a good idea
to do heroin and then mow the lawn unless he has a
quality mower. a poor-quality mower can potentially
detract from the experience of a good heroin high.
regardless, this is all very curious. my lawn boy
also looks like a young leonardo decaprio. that is, if
decaprio were from north central indiana and did
heroin. i suppose the yard boy jo h could resemble
decaprio in *the basketball diaries,* though that film
depicts new york in the 1990s. jo h showed up to
my house last week, my girlfriend opened the door,
and jo h asked, "is **he** here?" jo h does not know my
name i don't think. he calls me "he," which pleases
me. on this occasion, jo h asked if he could borrow
my mower to mow another house. i said "fine," and i
did not see my mower nor jo h for three days, which
is also fine. jo h left his blue cruiser bicycle on my
front lawn, and i enjoyed riding the cruiser. three
days later i was driving my car, and i noticed jo h
mowing another person's lawn. jo h: "i will drop your

mower off later." me: "okay, you know you left your bicycle at my house?" jo h: "i did? which one?" me: "the blue one." after running errands i returned to my place of residence. my lawn mower was in the middle of my lawn, the blue cruiser bicycle gone, and in its place a skateboard. jo h only utilizes one vehicle at a time, which i admire. the other day i asked jo h how much heroin he likes to do at one time, and he replied "as much as it takes." "fair enough," i said. lately, i've been riding the skateboard around the neighborhood and to work. i am getting pretty good at it. my lawn is due for another trimming. i wonder if jo h will bring over rollerblades.

progress

in the future
i imagine teenagers
walking around with handguns
they doubly use as phones

this way
they can talk to a friend,
say "hold on
one minute, larry"
and then shoot
someone
for doing
something
or nothing

they could film
their homicides
maybe
snapchat their heroics
of civic duty

all criminals.
all heroes,
what's the difference?

and that's
right

the popular
name
of countless
teenagers
in the
future
will be
larry

robby richard

seventh grade
speech class
robby richard

(which you pronounced
re-shard
like the french do
even though we were in texas
and robby had never
been out of the state
and lived with his nineteen year-old sister
and her boyfriend
in a trailer
and had no real ties
to the frogs
that we knew of)

yeah robby
got up
in front of class
for his pantomime
assignment
of a "familiar activity"
he licked
the imaginary paper
stuck the ends
together
after putting
an invisible

pinch of something
down
started to roll
the thing
in an imaginary
though convincing way

our teacher
mrs carlisle
stopped him
before he could raise
the creation
to his lips
"that's enough robby"
she said

the rest of us
wanted to
see the completion
of ingenuity

(though some students
had no idea how
the pantomime
was going to end
and were doubly confused)

a few of us
had been
over to robby's
trailer
had seen the sister
and boyfriend
partake

in this very activity
countless times
in an
unimaginary way

back at
his desk
robby was
upset

on some level
he knew he had
done something wrong
but on another level
and i agreed with him
he was
per the assignment
merely recreating
a simple activity that
was familiar

the joint
was imaginary
how can you get in trouble
for your imagination?

years later
i thought about this
when another friend
(named lee
after the general)
called in a fake bomb
at the high school

lee
he was found out and
got suspended
for three weeks
even got taken down
to the police station
had to get some expensive
lawyer

these days
they say imagination is dead
and maybe they are right
best to roll fat joints
and make actual bombs
for your lips and enemies

if you asked robby
he would say
that trailer was real
as were the lives
of his sister and her boyfriend
while the parents were
long gone

if you asked robby
he would say all of
that stuff was
just too heavy to
bring to school
a fake joint
you can
put in your pocket
tuck it safely

away from
trailers and seeing
too much
too soon

and i hear
robby is in jail now
i know
i haven't imagined it
maybe i have
maybe i choose to

maybe i choose
to roll
these things
with my mind
authorities be damned
authorities
paperless
in my fingers
these invisible explosions

this shit is real
and familiar too
you know that
maybe not

maybe you
read with machines
and amphetamines

yeah
amphetamines
in a corporate church

here's to you home town

where were you houston
when i was in broomfield
and westminster
denver
as a lonekid
in a school of angelic gangs spotted bandannas
and fistfights walking downhill through the frost
boulder
next door mountains
cold air slicing my eyes
disjointed ill thoughts on my mind

when dad took a gun to egypt
arrested in egyptian prison
beaten like a man on dirt floors
mom got the call
sat us down and said
alteration is reality

when i was in okc
in the bible belt thinking i was the devil
awkward teenager thinking pure nasty thoughts
drinking beer and everclear on the backroads
calling girls who had no idea
dad drunkenly flipping his car
going wrong way on one-way roads

when in indiana
chaz took too many pills
broken hospitals
stealing chairs and setting them on fire
all night in jails
with poison milk

when i was in australia
puking blood out of taxi cabs thinking pregnancy
and losing my cerebrum in the outback

when in bali
breaking into pool bars
paying off policemen

when in northern california
living in a shack surfing cold waters
working overtime and guessing the truth
about my father and neighbors

and where are you houston
now that i am two and a half hours west of you
crying and singing your name?

jo h: part 3

was walking lloyd round the neighborhood. a man in a new-looking ocean blue toyota corolla pulled up. "you see a white car speed down here? he hit somebody down there, ran through two lights." i told him i hadn't. lloyd and i walked on. two blocks away we saw a young man in red shirt, baggy jeans, being handcuffed by a police officer. an older man, white shirt, pontificating wildly to another officer in the yard. i noticed the white car, all smashed in the front. the young man being handcuffed, his pants started to fall down below his cheeks, grey underwear exposed. funny moment: the officer grabbed the young man's pants, pulled them up, and held them there while he pushed the young man towards the police car. the other man, the one in the white shirt, pontificated even wilder. i yelled out: "you know jo h?!" the handcuffed young man shook his head. the other cop told me: "sir, you need to move along." lloyd decided to pee in the lawn. "the beast wants what the beast wants," i said. "move along, please." i saw the man with the corolla down the road. he had a duck dynasty-type beard and one missing front tooth. i hate to say duck dynasty. i don't think this man watches reality television. he: "guess they got the guy." "guess so," i said. "can't believe it," he said. "can't believe what?" "i can't believe the cops did what they said they was gonna do." "do they not usually?" "shit. never usually. 'cept a couple times."

today: to do

          i could go to the
grocery store
          shower
          i could
          fill out the form
          to consolidate my debt
          mail it in

          i could work on a job
application for
          subway sandwiches
          pack for the road-trip
          few days away
          make phone calls
          work on crap novel
          read
          meditate
          simplify my life
          i could put a bullet
through my temple
          maybe the back of
my throat

          i could do all of it
          just check them off
          one by one

my hometown (or, the town where i pay 1/2 the rent on a home)

1

they say axl rose lived
in lafayette indiana
for the first 17 years
they also say axl
is now crazy and delusional

i am not going to start a band

2

i drank a bottle of
whiskey
took a bunch of pills
woke up
played tennis

3

this super tuesday
promises to be the best
super tuesday since
the last super tuesday
two weeks ago

jo h: part 17

jo h came over today on his blue cruiser bicycle.
it did not have a chain, which i asked him about.
"bike's busted." "how do you ride it?" i asked. "i ride
it only downhill." "why don't you just walk?" "i hate
walking." "what happened to your skateboard?"
"a car busted it. snapped it in two." those dreams,
it seems, are dead. i asked jo h about his heroin
hobby. "trying to say 'no' to all the things i used
to say 'yes' to. but, this other day i was in bed and
this son-of-a-bitch put a needle in my arm." "what
did you do?" "busted him in his teeth." "what did
he do?" "i called the cops, told them what he did."
jo h bummed a cigarette off me. "just trying to say
'no' when i used to say 'yes,'" he repeated. i didn't
mention the cigarette. he did a poor job on my lawn
this time. a poorer job than usual. i hate to mention
it, but he did a better job when he was on heroin.
maybe that dream is dead too.

hole

early morning at donut place listening to four old
men shoot the breezy shit:

"lucian there has a motorcycle with a bunch
of green lights on it."

"five dollars per light. spent about twelve
thousand dollars on those lights."

"got tipped off by frank in lebanon [indiana].
he's got a bunch of red lights on his."

"we knew you had lost your mind."

"you got a grandson?"

"one in texas. he's ornery, spoiled. won't
even mow the yard."

"my grandson is 16, his dad doesn't let him
mow the yard."

"kids today so lazy. ain't doing 'em any
favors."

"that george bush looks the same now don't
he?"

"same as he did when he was a kid. you know it's him."

"he's a good old boy ain't he?"

"better than the muslim we got now."

these four old men at this donut place are watching a documentary playing on an old television in the corner about the bush family dynasty. it's six in the morning. i pay the $2.36 for my donut and coffee. 1950s prices in indiana. all else. they say the elderly are supposed to be wise. full of wisdom and all that. but these old balls here are just a bunch of . . . oh, well, you know what they say: don't focus on the hole in the donut.
maybe i'll get some green lights for the motorcycle i can't afford. maybe i'll mow my yard for a change, drive to lebanon.

i am a texan

for allen ginsberg

i am a texan
i do not raise my lonestar to the death penalty

i am a texan
the suburbs make me puke chorizo in my mouth

i am a texan
my guns are buried 190 feet below the alamo
i throw my bullets into the gulf

i am a texan
my father works for big oil and gas
i ride a bicycle to buy rubber bullets
shoot *dallas* billboards in south padre island

i am a texan
i am a libertarian
my liberties include the right to
give away my possessions
expose myself at willie nelson's picnic
swim in mcconnaughey's pool while he attends
longhorn football
steal lance armstrong's expired bicycle
wear rick perry's eyeglasses at a gay bar
dope my own blood with fiesta vegetables the red
blood cells of capitol pacifists

i am a texan
i have earned the right
to steal a george w bush painting
i sneak border crossers with my mind
i do not apologize for eating vegan
breakfast tacos at the steakhouse
i am a texan
i move across the regions and topography
of this vast state on foot
my lone star is a lotus position

my lone star is a sad meditation into my beer
i am a texan
my capital punishment takes place
in the austin public library
i am a texan
i am a pacifist
i am not sorry
i am a texan
sam houston gave me a blowjob
stephen f austin gave me a rim job
i am a texan
i use a bowie knife to make salad
i am a texan
davie crockett has been reincarnated
in the form of a poodle
that licks the peanut butter off my taint
i am a texan
i am not sorry my lone star
is a thousand thoughts about harming no one
in the hill country
my terrorists are made of wax
they are in museums
i am not sorry

move to oklahoma if you are upset
thump your bible
when i put your gun up my ass
pull the trigger for you to see
what a texan's brain matter
looks like at your feet

and yeah
i'm a texan

i do not apologize

3 seattle poems

1: a thousand dreams

bohemia is dead
but i am at the bauhaus coffee shop
two older gentlemen
walk holding hands
young lady writes
poem in notebook

corner
water drinker
eying grocery boy
i sip coffee
with a thousand dreams
of experimentalists
who have taken wrong turns
in search of the bardo
maybe a city block
for hedonists

art may
or may not
be an excuse
in this metropolis
a vehicle
for deferment
the downright

with few exceptions
for trying

what the
visceral realists
put forth

2: vacation

i recently realized i work
as a manny
on the same street as the house
kurt cobain shot himself in

it makes me want to call in sick
break up with my person
move to portland
or vietnam
somewhere like that
with buddhists
in beach resorts
who torch themselves
in the spirit
of idealism

wait
do they?

besides
who would watch
the children?

3: humbling

i understand
the only other job kurt cobain
had was as a janitor

i only imagine
what type of janitor
he was

the below par kind

long smoke breaks
short attention to the urinals

whoever was in charge
probably didn't fire him
out of pity
some kind of agreement
a filial punk duty

jesus

a janitor

i will never look at
another janitor the same
i will never look at you the same
as i clean the shit streaks
out of my toilet
and grab lloyd's feces
with my hands

now

trying to read eckhart tolle's
power of now
but the only powerful nowness
i feel is this cramped apartment
this depressed dog
that needs to be
walked in the rain
the constant back pain i have
the crippling astronomical debt
i am hoping to avoid
the reality that the construction sounds
next door are jarring enough
to knock any diligent zen master off his mat

(try meditating through that)

no

i don't think there's much
power of now
as you feel your leg get
blown off in the gulf war
as you stick your finger up
your dog's ass
to secrete his anal glands

the hot death squirting on your boot

the only now i have
is to crack open this cheap beer
close eckhart's book
and think about a time
i've never imagined
a time before anal glands
and gulf wars
before scriptures and sounds
of manmade gods

right to unbear

i will give you your guns if you give me my abortions. i say we set up gun clinics wherein we can only buy our guns. if a person decides to buy a gun then s/he has to, upon walking into the gun clinic, wade through all of the radical protesters with pamphlets, poster signs/placards and yells of "thou shalt not kill! – exodus 20:13"; "thou shalt not kill; and whosoever shall kill shall be in danger of judgment! – matthew 5:21"; "thou shalt not kill! – deuteronomy 5:17"; "and he that killeth any man shall surely be put to death! – leviticus 24:17"; "for all they that take the sword shall perish with the sword! – matthew 26:52"; "whoever strikes a man so that he dies shall be put to death! – exodus 21:12." also, before you shoot someone in the chest or say the neck for breaking into your house you would have to watch a fuzzy monitor, see that person's heart beating on the small black and white screen. this is freedomness after all. the right to bear arms and placards. the right to unbear uteruses filled with goo. the right to graffiti scripture on the atheist parlors of our minds. our minds and minds' eyes. forever. forever. amen. travis. randy. george. straight.

a poem on guilt

you may go
        berserk
throw your older brother's
        flat screen television
through his back
        apartment window

and yes his laptop
        his lava lamp
into spiderweb glass
        sprawling patterns

        dents in the floor

        you may even smash
the guitar he never plays

you may wonder why
        you did this
why you've lost it
        you will go through
those revolutions
        in your mind
recall the past horror beneath

it will add up
        and it will not
you will be afraid

of what you are
capable of
of the need to see
the surface of things
obliterated

this will terrify you
yes it will
but at least you will then
know
at least you
have a chance
to live another snap

because you did not
go back to his house
for destroying his property
and he did not
kill you
with the pistol
he said he was going
to shoot you with

at least
you are alive
prepared to try
prepared to shed
the metal
of familiarity
in healthier ways

that's something
you tell
yourself

another poem on guilt

i feel guilty
            when i admit
i like pablo escobar

i watch a documentary
            film about him
and a fictional television show

            i like the plump
                        man
who killed thousands
            who aided
            in getting millions addicted

                        a type
            of columbian robin hood
                        they say
            beloved
                        in medellin especially

i don't know

            when he smiles
                        for his mugshot
      i smile
            then feel i should
go to church

something
to show penance
for watching so much television

celebrating
fantods
phantoms inside
the box
of my checkered
heart

but then
again
my brother's television
is dead

c list

been thinking
about the overlooked pear

getting short shrift
compared to the more
popularly consumed fruits

the banana
orange
famous household
apple
exotic mango

but at times the
apple is too tart

the pear can work
better
in a cake or pie
cobbler

appreciated sustenance
like the siblings of a more
well-known celebrity

tom hanks's brother jim
ron howard's brother clint
chad lowe maybe preferable
to rob

the poor pear doesn't
                  get the press
      barely a mention in the magazines
but where would we be without
                  someone like clint howard?
                  who would die
      in all the movies?

                  who would take the bullets
                        for the more
      glamorous fruit

                  the ones
                              responsible for
            the posters on
                  your bedroom walls
                              the ones
            you get naked to
                        in your minds

      your dreams
with few shapes
      like pears?

literary theory

had a conversation with ernest hemingway, told him: "so, i was speaking with a graduate student in american studies. she says you hate women, that your work is the product of a sad latent homosexual." he almost laughed. "but, what about it?" i asked. "is that true?" "no," he said. "i wish it were that easy. i hate some women same as men." "so . . . you're a misanthrope," i said. "jesus, i don't hate all people. hate and love? too difficult to tell the difference mostly." "so you simultaneously love and hate all people?" "jesus. i need a drink. you make me want to shoot myself. just tell your friend not to worry about it. i don't hate her. why would i? i have never met her." "she sure does hate you though," i said. "screw it," ernest said. "she probably just needs to get laid." "see . . . that right there," i said. "she would take issue with that." "isn't this your poem?" he asked. "isn't this your fiction?" "yeah, but i would never say that. the critics would hate it." "political correctness is for the birds," he said. "birds? is that a derogatory euphemism for women? a hegemonic way of asserting your dominance?" "what?" he said. "i just mean birds. jesus, i can't say anything." "and when you say jesus is that supposed to be ironic or atheist?" "i hate you." "does that mean you love me?" "no, it means you are annoying. now buy me a drink." "do you want me to buy you a drink because you are anti-feminist?" and, then, ernest took out his shotgun and blew his head off. he finally realized he wanted to die. the birds were not singing.

conservation

save the planet
save yourself!
maybe i have
seen it all

behind the display
glass at this local
coffee shop
it just beamed there
like excalibar or
something glamorous
like that

WATER IN A BOX!

what would the
native americans
think about this
boxed water?
would they
sell it at the casino?
would they
take their boxes of water
into peyote dens
hallucinate
rid their spirits
while asking

"kindness, will
you hand me my
boxed water?"

boxes
are better
than
plastic bottles
we know that
i am going to take
a toilet filled
with water
lug it
to downtown
seattle
just before
the work rush
make a sign
that says

TOILET WATER
ONLY A NICKEL
A DRINK

this would *save the planet*
clear our consciences
they could sell it
at casinos
on cruise ships
for the lame

it's all a
      goddamned cliché
         a racket anyway
     sure yeah
       i hear
           people pay for
             oxygen

             in los angeles

america

i drive my japanese compact
through oregon twilight and what thoughts
            i have of you, allen ginsberg:
where does your beard point tonight?

did you ever imagine this current
                candy-corn imperialism
of orange gorilla warfare?

would you give me pills for this
                perpetual spine pain,
        this bipartisan rigmarole
in the name of tribal fallacies?

would you realize the faulty currents of
                our blind bat-shit enumerations,
        or would you,
                old courage
                teacher, keep driving
        through the greenery,
                bypassing pnw communist meetings
                and pseudo-constitutional   frater-
nity banquets; would you log in
                with a golden password
                for anti-cyber warfare,
        realize the enemy was in our hearts,
                        a sick lower 48

of unloved incestuous wordplay?
how much are those bananas?
how much would you pay
to scorch this earth, rid these tortured
people of their automated
grocery stores — their long lines of credit
& neon hate crimes   dis-
guised as porcelain tweets:

these broken reiterations littered
across this fallen road,
our collective fog lights disabled
to the feet of giants?

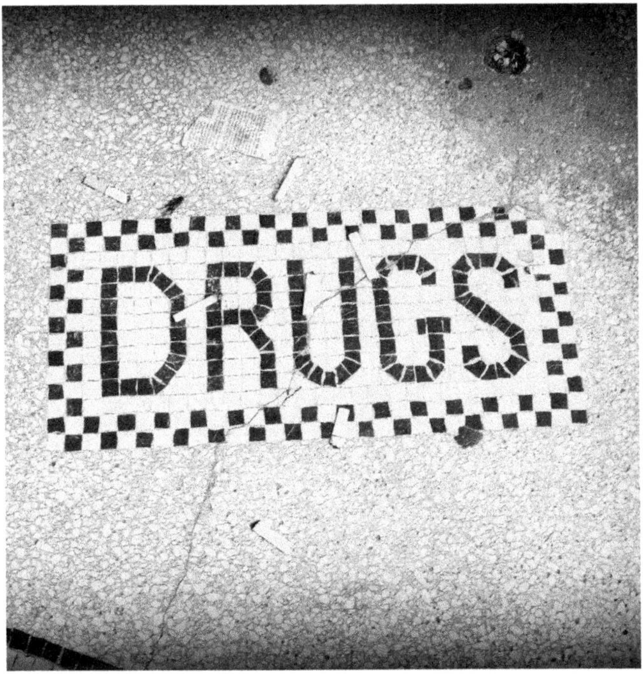
DRUGS

a brooklyn moon

a time i was doing
a lot of cocaine and
other shit in brooklyn
bathrooms late twenties
my whole world was
all-you-can-eat oysters

in the bathroom
one dive
i inhaled bumps like
maximus with a guy named *spank*
a drugdealer who looked samoan
though when i asked about his history
he replied: "i am just from the land of
spank. beginning and end"

we carried on like that
through a few shifts of the
moon landing until finally
i felt something like guilt
like i needed to move past
the middle man of the illicit
enterprise for privileged
and sad consumers

in spank's extended van
with two other men we were going
on a run we stopped

at government housing
a highrise close to the
brooklyn-queens expressway
i took a package from
spank's hand said i would do
it up take it up
up the six flights of
stairs synthetic
hallway lights residual furniture
and bags of potato chips
on the worn-down feet of doors

a woman answered one door:
"you got what i want?" she asked

i looked behind her in the apartment
two small children one in a diaper
crying and that world opened
then closed like a can of expired tuna

"there's been a mistake"
i said turning
and walking fast down
the stairs back into
the van into the night
that had lost all
virginity
if there
ever was

"i couldn't do it"
i said to spank
"if it was just her
that would be fine

but a crying kid?
no way"

spank pulled a
handgun out
from the van console
pointed it
toward the dash
it just resting there
like a mongoose
in hawaii

"you need to go back
up there" he said
i looked at him
his non-samoan seriousness
"i just can't" i said
he held me hard
by the shoulder
squeezed until there was
a pain
sure yes there was

and he laughed
we laughed
and stayed like that
until the cows came
until the cows
came home to that
brooklyn moon
and i was ready
to drink cheap beer again
to piss in my own bathroom again

hold that package like
it was air like it was
now something that
had grown out of
fashion out and past
me at least for the night
at least for that time just
that once i had done
something decent
for someone else
not thinking about
my moon but the
fallen stars of others
that were never
there in the first place

at least i had
no business
looking to that
sky
that one time

machines

it's mlk's birthday
i'm watching
a disney cartoon
about john henry
with a four-year-old

the kid points
to a hole in my sock
i tell him socks' holes
are best
he puts a small
rock collection
on my other foot
but john henry?

fighting
the industrial
revolution
not being a
serf to machines?
i get
the point
but i also
realize i've
been watching
cartoons
with this kid

for four hours
instead of
babysitting
teaching him how
to read
or building something
i've let the television's
hypnosis
do the work

no
john henry would
not be happy
about this
especially not on
mlk day
especially not as
depicted by the
not so virtuous
disney

can't wait
until the next
holiday

maybe i can
commit a hate crime
on valentine's

on healthy love

only loved
        three women

really loved them
        a few others
i projected jv love towards
           junior varsity love

but three women
call it varsity love

        the first i was young
           she was young we
        didn't even have a name
for the moon

the second i was drunk
        she was drunk
           we got our car stuck
in mud on a hill
           in mexico and i took
              it as a marker
        for future fuck ups
and impossibilities

        but this one
        the third one
        makes the best sense

she runs marathons
        uphill and i chain smoke until i feel
like i don't want to die and we meet
                somewhere along the road
        in that middle ground of
                    functionality
            where love
        actually makes you
                    want to clean the
                    dishes because
            tomorrow you think
        you might realistically
            use them pour
        coffee into a mug
                you both use in the morning

trophy room

            a bar called
        shorty's

            an entrance that says
        "trophy room"
            flickers

            the neon clown next to the
        entrance light flickers
            the clown's large thumb
        and cigar
            alternating light

            all for the entrance
        to the trophy room
            which is actually a room filled
with vintage pinball machines
            those machines
        insignia
            for victory
        of leisure

            i do not think they played pinball
in vietnam
            not in
guantonomo

                    i think terrorists
          should play pinball
                    war criminals
          bingo!
                    the added
          rushes of adrenalin
                    could clean the waters
          clear the air
                    make death
          seem like a perfect score
                    next to the brilliant
                              ferocious lights
                    silver balls

          putin pinball
mother teresa pinball
          gandhi pinball
bin laden pinball
          saddam pinball
                    yes
          i want to
                    play a saddam hussein pinball
          machine see
                    the lights over
          baghdad
                    listen to the clang
          of palace doors
                    pinball for
          world hunger
                    pinball for
          diplomacy!

oh well

          i never actually
make it back
          to the trophy room
to see if
          what is what
it's too loud back there
          too crowded
with aggressive people
          slapping each other
on the backs
          like it's some
kind of game
                    for trophies

technology

the sun was out in seattle, and i was enjoying the rays like a ball tickle from the gods. on my way to the capitol hill neighborhood i noticed a gutterpunk kid standing in the middle of the street blocking traffic. up close i noticed the kid was female. she yelled out to another gutterpunk kid, a teenage boy, after she had caused him to run across the street: "i am going to kill you, boy! you better run away!" the boy backtracked, with his arms spread like christ, across the street to confront her. she yelled again and pointed at his face: "you tried to steal my phone!" she pulled out a smart phone, one of the expensive kind. "trying to rob me, boy!" and i thought to myself: her phone is nicer than my phone, and i then recalled a time i walked up to a coffee shop not too long ago, also in seattle, to use the internet. a seemingly homeless gutterpunk guy on the corner yelled out to me: "hey, man, you want to check your email for a dollar?!" this gutterpunk had a laptop out on the sidewalk. "sure," i said. "a dollar for internet is cheaper than buying coffee at this place."

the two gutter royals here were still yelling at each other. the prince being verbally attacked also pulled out his phone, a very nice smart screen type. "i have a phone!" he yelled. "why would i want to steal yours?!" as i thought about my crap flip phone that i pay 31 dollars a month for, the gutterpunk queen threw a brick at the kid that hit him in the chest. "this has been a strange day," a homeless guy draped in rainbows of blankets said to me. we were on the corner. i could have gone either way. "i know," i said. "i need a nicer phone. blend in with the leisure class." he pulled a bright blanket over his face. the sun was out and on and on.

my rent is stuck

on the ceiling
of the comet tavern
            is about 800 dollars
worth of bills
            just stuck there
some crumpled
            some nearly
hovering just below
                        the tiles

            the fans blow on
them shifting
            them subtly like
sunflowers
            in a field
                        somewhere else

            somewhere i
                        can't afford
to travel to

religion

as a kid i went to the summit, the old houston rocket's nba basketball arena, and not long ago i visited that same stadium off i-59. after parking my car in the large spiraling lot, i walked with the other fans to the arena. atm machines everywhere, and in the same slots where i used to spy all-star center akeem "the dream" olajuwon jerseys and other rockets memorabilia, i saw the visage of a slick-oiled haircut and a beaming grin of too white castles.

joel osteen!

the leader/christian minister of the world's largest mega church—his face on books, posters, t-shirts, cd's, much else.

at my seat in the arena i could see and hear a christian rock band, having been flown in from australia—a laser light show, billows of fog smoke, and then—of course—joel's large mug on massive screens, maybe 10,000 people standing up arms raised, beaming down on their hero, with unbridled faith and enthusiasm. "it's god's will for you to live in prosperity instead of poverty," said joel. "it's god's will for you to pay your bills and not be in debt."

it seems i was the only one still sitting down, trying

hard not to puke in my mouth—the horror, joel (!) the horror. taking my mind away from the immediate spectacle i thought about what i had witnessed in this same arena as a kid wherein akeem olajuwon earned the added 'h' to his name to indicate a king-god's status. hakeem then more regally presented, i also thought of

hjoel osteen!

hjoel almost ryhmes with (looks like) "hole"—as in the hole in my heart, the breaking of my heart for a simpler time, a period of fewer moral conflicts, an equally capitalistic time but one of fewer hypocrisies, my own.

having seen enough, i left hjoel's sermon early, exiting and leaving the legion of ecstatic christians to fill their own holes in relative non-peace. on the way out i drew some cash from one of the atm machines. i wanted to get breakfast maybe go play shuffleboard or to the rothko chapel. yes, the rothko chapel. at the rothko chapel i could meditate on non-denominational nothingness, try to shed the repetitive jerk-off film strip of hjoel's unreal white incisors polluting my mind. and, i wonder what hakeem is doing right now? i wonder if he needs a congregation, a following, another stadium. i would attend it, i really would, and i would stand up, happily raise my arms to him. it's a faith, and i still have his jersey. because i was there. i was a witness. i was a kid and he was my god. my first and only. the only one i paid for.

conversation overheard smoking circle front of unicorn bar, seattle

here he is back from the drunk tank

or sleeping on a roof

i slept in my bed for once, it didn't feel right

probably had to rip the plastic off it

the movie with sean penn and madonna, shanghai hustle

worst movie in the world

we did whip-its this morning as we watched it

it can't be as fucked up as the golf channel, these golfers miss a shot and they psychoanalyze it: "well, he would have made that putt if he wasn't molested as an eleven-year-old"

he would have won that round if he hadn't of found out his mom wasn't his mother at the age of 24

if he hadn't of realized his mother wasn't his father

shit, me and lucien went to the park, were fighting mma style, I suplexed him backwards into the turf bet his back is a crow bar today

nah he works on an alaskan fishing boat, tough
motherfucker, he'll be fine

good to see you guys

pleasure

gentlemen

social media in old age

what are we going to do
about the facebook in
my your
70s and beyond?

people dying
dead people sick
their pictures
profiles then
who is going to
delete their profiles?
who will have all
the passwords?
what does this
facebook
look like for an
older person?

constant reminders
of death disease
deformed
grandchildren
arthritis cirrhosis
of the liver

here's a photograph
or a video

of larry not
drinking in
cabo san lucas
or larry
not walking around
just in bed checking
blood pressure
here's larry's new
bed pan
or here's a post
from judy
she has no memory
no mind really
of yesterday's post

no i should cut
out that facebook
social media
altogether
because it's going
to get sad

glad your hemmorhoids
have cleared up
larry thumbs up
i like that a lot

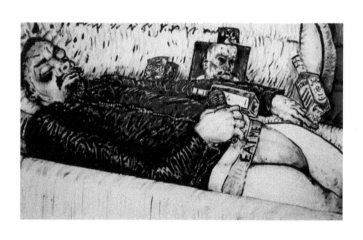

family history

i got into a bar fight
in ireland

this is true

the four cousins
and i
along with our
temporary nemeses
trickled out
into the street
pretending to be
waterfalls

i hit the guy
in his mouth
an incisor
cutting my knuckle
and i fell
backward
another guy
an irishman
jumped on top
hit me on the side
of the head
my cousin john ross
a lanky texan

who works off
the gulf shore
punched him
in the bull's eye
that was
the center
of his face

the fight
continued
like this
the irishmen
retreated bloodied
and tired
us a tad
less so
two cousins
had their
shirts off
one yelled
"T-E-X-A-S!"

back at the
quaint bed and
breakfast of this
otherwise quiet
town in central
ireland
my cousins
were revved
up rearing for
more else
as my one
cousin michael

a nurse-in-training
at the local college
popped my
left shoulder
back in place

the old lady
of the b&b
kicked us
out but
not before
another cousin
philip puked
a foul
jameson signature
over white sheets

my aunt penny
woke up
in the next room
penny
a lovely
tough woman
who has
outlived many men
woke up
put us
in the
tight van
she insisted
on driving

"texas forever"
one cousin said

"fish and
chips please"
said another

and this
was true

my hand
shattered
shoulder
shot
i wanted
to go
see something
beautiful
closer to
the water
the healing
elements
of our irish
great grandparents
before they
migrated
to texas
before cross-atlantic
sacrifices
were made
before
the crossing

before any
violence
to write about

relativity

sure size matters
        but not always
        how you think

goldie locks
got down with
the just right bear
        a big gulp is too
                        much
and sure
        that horse
                cock
might make
        you walk funny
and there's
        the american
                military
switzerland
has no military
        haven't seen
                any soundbites
                        about their
                                inferiority complex
        miniature poodles
                seem to be celebrated
yes texas
        is a big state
                they are proud of that

but alaska
        is bigger
no one really
        seems to care
                buffets are often
                        too much
diarrhea
the tallest building
        in dubai
                pretty gratuitous
                        in the desert
                                it's vast already
sure
big shit
all feces
indoor plumbing
seems
just right

olympia

washington a
woman cries
yells
sitting down
on the concrete
outside
the fence
of this bar's
side patio

her voice is broken glass:

*i can't even have the shoes that were on his feet
dude fuck this town people are so fake here bunch
of fucking freeloaders sit around doing nothing for
nobody bunch of losers in this fucking fantasy world
why are you here? i am fucking done i have had 45
years of suffering like i don't have a right to what he
was wearing when he fucking died give me a fucking
break where do you people come from? i don't know
who these people are where they fucking come from
oh my god it's fucking tiring and i have a goddamn
right a goddamn right to have the shoes that kurt
cobain died in! why are these people here they are
like the fucking baby on the nirvana cover! i mean
really why are they here? they are inconsiderate to
every person that walks by what is their problem
why are they here why is this guy living above this*

*bar for two years i came here to get a job and i walk
on the sidewalk and i get murdered every day these
people don't like nirvana they don't like kurt cobain
they fucking shit on francis cobain they hate the rock
band they have no respect for his life or his family
what do you do with your life? what did you people
ever do with your life they sit here every fucking day
badmouthing kurt cobain and courtney love like the
people who live here hate nirvana and why are they
here they don't know me no wonder he went and
shot and killed himself these are the same people
that murdered him and they sit here and freeload
off his fucking life why are you here? why are you
talking about me sir i don't even know who you are
no i don't live in total insanity and neither did kurt
cobain who the fuck are you? this guy above the bar
needs to go into a fucking psyche ward and i am not
fucking kidding you did marco kill kurt cobain? is
that why he's sitting here raping his family all day
who are you people who the fuck are you people? i
think he murdered kurt cobain david david this guy's
been sitting here for four fucking years david i think
marco murdered kurt cobain i think he really did!*

i finish my beer

leave the bar
walk around
outside
the fence
to get
a look at this woman

she approaches me

"excuse me sir do you have
a cigarette you could spare?"

so polite
fairly well put
together mid forties
she has been talking to herself
no marco or david
or anyone else
in sight

i don't know what to make of this
olympia washington   kurt cobain
conspiracy theories
rage-filled
maybe schizophrenia
gutter punks playing music in the street
dogs napping by their sides

morrisey plays out the bar's speakers
nwa plays
patsy cline sings

at a vegan restaurant now
next door
cyndi lauper
croons about true colors
i wonder who cyndi
was singing to

maybe it's to this woman out there
along with marco and david
and anyone else

people behind me
talk about
writing

& writers:
"i think one of his books
he wrote
about how to write"

"yeah it's called *on writing*"

"one of his books drags out"

"i have to go to the bathroom
which is the ladies'? i can't tell"

"both"

"is this lgbtq friendly?
i identify
with the men's bathroom
i like the short lines"

people laugh
cyndi lauper
people in a booth
speak:

"our struggle is real"

"all of my favorite rock stars
have died this year"

"david bowie
prince
scott weiland
my roommate"

"merle haggard"

"he was a redneck
but he was a rock star"

"how the hell is
keith richards
still alive?"

"i thought he would be
dead at 55"

"i have had my driver's
license since '91 but i
haven't had a car
the reason is i don't
want to get a d.u.i."

anyway
why are you here?

olympia
are you there?

marco?
david?

anybody?

cyndi?

why are you
here?

who are you?

who   the   fuck   are   you   people?

pacifism

at the twilight
exit

bar two men
who look
like offensive
linemen play
shuffleboard
i can't imagine
the minor
crashes of the
pucks
meet their
testosterone needs
but then again
in the
twilight
electronic indie
music plays a
petite
man in jean
shorts with
a skinny
mustache
carries his
melon margarita to the back
patio

that is littered

       with idealists

no

       shuffleboard
       is the most

aggressive

       act at this bar
       a bar fight
       might as well
       be science

fiction

       or like
       bigfoot
       juggling

human

       heads that
       have recently
       been set
       on fire

moniker of a champion:
sitting next to sad bros

watching the olympics
table tennis on television
at a bar
i see ding ning hit
the small white ball with
her paddle to win the
gold medal for china

oh glory

a guy at the bar says
"they should have
named her ding dong
that would have been something"

another onlooker remarks
"my friend dated
a guy named ping pong"

other guy:
"they should have named her
mabel dennis"

jesus

these guys

that ding

meditation

the time has come
the time came
the time never was
the was was never time

middle way

top 40 poetry seems so dense
overly esoteric confusing
the opposite of top 40 radio
yet equally dispiriting

the radio makes me stupid
top 40 poetry makes me feel stupid

i am not a buddhist per se
but today i seek the middle way
those poems and songs
accessible in their beauty wisdom
their offerings that make me better
make me hopeful and willing
to believe enlightenment
is not just another bumper sticker
$8.95 at the vintage
yin yang store
not just
another
precious whisper
on npr

**jo h once told me a joke
tween yard spells**

"hey
why did the
cow with breast cancer
forget your birthday?"

"why?"

"she had no
mammary"

where did
you go
jo h?

where have you
been?

and lloyd

lloyd says hello
something like:

HI, HOW ARE YOU

my lungs are a dive bar

in this postlapsarian state
i see appendages
unhinged from bodies

amid sawdust floors makers
mark arrangements

broken johnny
walker eyeglasses
secured with medical tape

a bartender on the nod

within myself i see the
asbestos we pray to

the windowless walls of
sunrise mourning

those forgiving ashtrays
replacing clergymen.

do you own your mind?
did you find those plastic
flowers in the attic
throw them away with
hopes of better
arrangements?

because all of the cocaine and
opioids have never gotten
that prize you're looking for.

you've never truly lingered
on this jukebox, this
kaleidoscopic neon carousel
of downbeat sparks
and illumination—

these fibrous cocktails
represent compasses,
concoctions of direction.
this map of degenerates that
we treat as saints,
these bar stools
occupied by stranger gods that,
with one eye cocked, stir you
towards polychrome celebration—

and for you:

for your collapsing pedigree,
a pbr and a landscape,

i speak my bearded graffiti jukebox:

my lies are encyclopedias
call my life a shelf

proved a melancholy time for the children
bathing raindrops off one another's tulips
into trash bags we never looked behind us

then saw hell in a toilet bowl

in portland maine
this town contains the casinos of our lives
we're left with pocket change of reckoning
pardon my fire the irony is that baudelaire
is fucking my roommate

alienation is a familiar postcard
i remember from childhood billboards

playing with food is like tonguing a rose

renewal isn't a place in idaho

don't take money from assholes
the interest is too high

calm in the sky is a distant friend now
who doesn't write letters longhand

homecoming is dregs
bad lies are dregs
fork in eye dregs
the clap dregs
mormons at door dregs
pee eye dregs
poison potato dregs
piercing nipple dregs
for three hours

constantly calling on angels
who have no boots

murder by numbers
never tried that

enter a contest for morality
vote for a priest
who doesn't eat hotdogs

living is the only familiar

a plan of nicer attack
where violence is a pomeranian

there's a rapist beside me
or so the waitress says

floating in the widening gyre
the maverick comes for her possessions

ah we stopped for the sake of non-denominations
and i saw loves shared by lifecroppers

flowers die
people stay the same

marry an elephant
for the sake of rooms

naked lady
opts to blowdry hair

california duped me
brought me back
once too many

i murdered the golden gate

a morning daisy
for the afternoon lunacy

on these days i play
imaginary games of table tennis
run til i need to smoke something
drink til i have no middle name
call the sister i don't have

the private and public realities
are killing our babies

memory only comes around
on the dance floor

a hitchhiker i picked up in my minivan told me
alaska would one day rain down nonsense
of ice pick terrorists
and scapegoats

give rice away
keep the beans for yourself

i would set myself on fire for the cause
if i knew how
but i never went to trade school
i never passed
the bill to that phantom in reno

a beggar once asked
if she could swallow my ribcage

meditated a thousand miles per second
realized i am a bridge

still here braving the beautiful absurd

forgive me
forgive yourself

you there?
                    do you want to buy one?
                            this graffitti music
                    on my mind—

            turn one
    into a
    movie

            or dreams for your nation?

*Gratuitous Photograph of Poet:

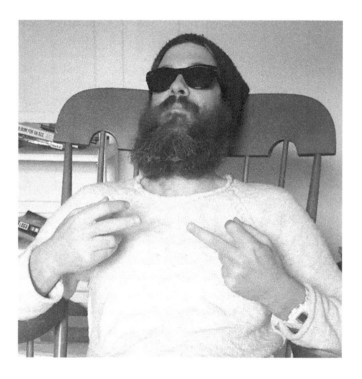

walter moore: ba. mfa. phd. cbd. thc. lived in about 20 towns/cities/countries, resided on street, in car, penthouse, condo, apartments, houses between, greyhounds. poet writer performer dancer sleeper friend partner. chainsmokes but plays table tennis at a professional level, enjoys secondhand papasan chair, treats roaches like fingers—drinks pea soup out of glass, buys cheap beer & steals expensive hot tubs, votes with waters and illuminates food trucks. his waterfall is an idea. teaches at oregon state university—and lives and plays in **corvallis**, oregon, with dog **lloyd** and lady friend **erica**.

*If you would like to contact Walt, bother him, ask him to read at your establishment for fun, and/or tell him he possesses fleeting moments of above averageness, please don't hesitate to email him at

moorewalterg@gmail.com

*Also check out Walt's poems (& readings of his poems) on his website at

www.waltermoorepoems.com

CPSIA information can be obtained
at www.ICGtesting.com
Printed in the USA
FSHW020459010419
56846FS